Joyce Jillson's™
Astrology for Dogs

By Joyce Jillson
Illustrated by Ronald Lipking

Irvine, California
A Division of BowTie, Inc.

Karla Austin, *Business Operations Manager*
Nick Clemente, *Special Consultant*
Jarelle S. Stein, *Editor*
Jennifer Perumean, *Assistant Editor*
Jill Dupont, *Production*
Janet Moir McCaffrey, *Book Designer*

Library of Congress Cataloging-in-Publication Data

Jillson, Joyce.
    Joyce Jillson's Astrology for dogs / by Joyce Jillson ; illustrator, Ronald Lipking.
        p. cm.
    ISBN 1-931993-30-0
    1. Astrology and pets. 2. Dogs--Miscellanea. I. Title.

    BF1728.3.J56 2005
    133.5'86367--dc22
                                                2004017005

BowTie Press®
A Division of BowTie, Inc.
3 Burroughs
Irvine, California 92618

Printed and bound in Singapore
10 9 8 7 6 5 4 3 2 1

to all my dogs in the world, especially my great danes, JUPITER, GEMINI, and NEPTUNE.

—joyce jillson

Joyce Jillson, internationally syndicated astrologer to the stars and major corporations, enjoyed life on a universal scale until her death, October 1, 2004.

Animals, from her three Great Danes, Jupiter, Gemini and Neptune; her many cats and in particular, her special 500-pound lion buddy, Donny, whom she led on a frail leash were Joyce's friends of choice. She believed they possessed psychic abilities enabling her to build relationships with them on a higher and more intimate level.

Joyce was not alone when she said, "Every creature has a unique chart, just as every pet has its own personality. We love each of them and cater to their strengths and frailties."

She's not alone now. We and her furry friends miss her already.

—Steve Adler

Contents

WHAT IS

DOG ASTROLOGY?

Introduction

D og astrology explains the metaphysical side of your dog and helps you understand his character and the ways he will interact with the world. Carl Jung studied astrology and believed the stars had a profound effect on the timing of events for people and animals. He called this the "universal connection." Studying dog astrology can help you better understand your furry significant other.

Astrology focuses on the zodiac, an imaginary heavenly belt extending to each side of the apparent path of the sun, including the paths of the moon and principal planets, except Pluto. The zodiac is divided into twelve equal sun signs, each named for a different constellation, and each marked by it's own symbol: **Aries** (The Ram), **Taurus** (The Bull), **Gemini** (The Twins), **Cancer** (The Crab), **Leo** (The Lion), **Virgo** (The Virgin), **Libra** (The Scales), **Scorpio** (The Scorpion), **Sagittarius** (The Horse), **Capricorn** (The Goat), **Aquarius** (The Water Bearer) and **Pisces** (Two Fish).

Each planet is part of a sun sign, which falls in one of four element groups: water, air, earth, or fire. Water sun signs include Cancer, Scorpio, and Pisces. Dogs of the water element tend to carry instinctive and sympathetic traits. Air signs include Gemini, Libra, and Aquarius. Dogs of these sun signs are often responsive and smart. Taurus, Virgo, and Capricorn are of the earth element, thus are full of ingenuity and persistence. Lastly, the fire element comprises Aries, Leo, and Sagittarius. These flaming sun signs are more approachable, tireless, and friendly.

Some dogs may be born on the cusp, which means that their birth dates fall during the transition from one sign to the next. This happens because the earth's journey around the sun take approximately $365\frac{1}{4}$ days, yet there are only 360 degrees in a circle. Thus the sun moves not one degree a day, but only about fifty-nine minutes a day. For example, each year the sun can enter Aries on any of the following days, March 19, March 20, March 21, or March 22. It all depends on the year. Most years, Aries starts on March 21.

The twelve categories of life, or mini-zodiac, are divided into houses similar to the zodiac's twelve symbols. These solar houses separate beings into twelve sections: individuality, finances, communications, home, creativity, improving daily life, relationships, transitions, personal growth, achievement, friendship, and the inner self. Your dog's Petrology Forecast is determined by a combination of his sun sign, houses, and planet positions.

Determining Your Dog's Birth Date

If you got your dog from a breeder or a friend, you know when the pup was born. Registration with the American Kennel Club requires a date of birth. But before you assume that these dates are accurate, assess the situation. Breeders may not remember correctly as often they may have two or more dogs who give birth around the same time.

Owners may want to have a professional astrologer draw their pets' charts because the miscalculation of just a few days can drastically affect the astrology chart. Accuracy is important to provide dog owners with more knowledge about how to love, train, and live with their animal partners.

Determining the precise birth date is also important for dogs born on the cusp of two signs. It's best for an astrologer to calculate your dog's exact time, date, and place of birth.

You might not be able to determine your dog's birth date. Not to worry. Celebrate Family Addition Day. The stars' alignment on this day can guide you in learning how to love, nurture, and live with your animal partner.

You can enhance your relationship with your dog by reading about all twelve signs to determine which appropriately describes your furry friend's astrological needs.

ARIES

March 21—April 19

The Aries Dog

Since ancient times, the first day of spring coincides with the first day of the Aries sign because early astronomers and calendar makers considered the year to begin on this date. Thus, Aries was designated as the first sign of the zodiac. When you get to know the Aries personality, you will understand why. Aries dogs are the quintessential leaders of the pack, and they'll make their presence known. They command, innovate, and discover new paths.

Your Aries dog has her own style. When she enters your household, you will adhere to a whole new set of rules. An Aries has particular sleeping and eating patterns. No matter how good the food, she'll let it sit in her bowl until she decides it's time to eat. Likewise, even a new toy will not keep her from sleeping if it's nap time.

An Aries is rambunctious and enthusiastic. You must never be unappreciative because she wears her emotions on her sleeve—or collar. Because she's so intense, she can easily become depressed, especially when you first check your message machine when you come home rather than celebrate her existence. She greets visitors with her usual bonhomie, so don't invite anyone over who isn't thrilled to make her acquaintance. For all you single romantics, an Aries will make snap judgments about who is—and isn't— a good partner for her beloved human companion. She will rush to meet your date, and if she's impressed, she'll

 jump with joy. If your pooch does not approve of your unfamiliar visitor, you'll notice in her eye a glimpse of the wild dog nature of her ancestors. Instead of her ususally warm, open-eyed face, she will display a challenging glint of disdain.

Being the great warrior of the zodiac, your Aries dog will fight for what she feels is right. The Aries may greet your apartment manager with glee in the hallway but see him as an intruder should he enter your premises unannounced. Advise the dog-sitter to immediately set out the dog food to avoid a nip from a hungry pup. Should there be a problem, it's probably the sitter's cologne—an Aries dog reacts subconsciously to any cheap fragrance.

An Aries dog is extraordinarily forgiving and are perfect companions for workaholic humans who may be gone all day—especially if you let them romp around like a jumping bean when you arrive home. In a full house, the Aries dog will show favoritism—but not toward the same person for all things. One will be the Aries' favorite television chum and the other her choice to run errands with. She will instinctively gravitate toward the person who best fulfills her needs at the given moment. This points out two of the Aries' best characteristics: expediency and efficiency. The Aries dog picks up clues about what you're thinking. When a lover lets you down, the Aries will notice your drooping shoulders even if there's a smile on your face.

Aries Pawcast

Symbol:
Ram, aggressive
and strong

Ruling planet:
Mars, the planet of intense emotion

Key personality trait:

An Aries pup is a trustworthy pal
and protective of her loved ones.

Would like more:
Attention. She can never
have enough. She loves
listening to you tell her
she's special. Be warned:
if she can't be the number
one good dog, she'll be the
number one bad dog, so
reward excellent behavior.

Dog idol:
wolf, fearless
and patient

Dreams and fantasies: An Aries dog would like to ride a motorcycle or drive a motorboat to get the thrill of the speed, but her ears are too sensitive to follow through with this fantasy. Instead she might try a skateboard or settle for riding shotgun with you in a Jeep (or if she's small, in the front basket of your bicycle like Toto from the *Wizard of Oz*).

Dating style: Hot to trot. She's ready to roll with the object of her affection as soon as he's in sniffing range. An Aries is very possessive and not shy about exhibiting her jealousy.

Best feature: an excellent guard dog

Worst feature: headstrong personality

Favorite entertainment: watching extreme sports on television

Favorite activity with owner: playing and sleeping

Pet peeves:

being ignored

Favorite food:
any morsel
not nailed
to the dish

Favorite thing about owner: your openness to new experiences and how you courageously take on the world

Favorite sport:
tennis ball toss

Mantra:

"Feet, do your thing."

TAURUS

April 20—May 20

The Taurus Dog

aurus is the second of the twelve signs of the zodiac, the one associated with money, assets, land, and natural talents. Your Taurus dog knows his value right from his first moments on the earth. Most likely he will have a prestigious pedigree. If he is not from champion stock, there will likely be something special about the circumstance of either where or when he was born to distinguish his birth. Perhaps his parents belonged to a well-known celebrity; maybe he came from an exotic location or has unusual, beautiful markings.

Rituals mean a lot to this dependable, composed pooch. The throat chakra (his center of spiritual energy) is of enormous importance to the Taurus dog. He'll sense tension in his throat, get thirsty sooner than other dogs, and growl with the intensity of a sonar boom. He has a golden voice. When he belts out an accompaniment to music it will be the canine equivalent of an operatic masterpiece. Don't ever get angry; this is his way of joining the party with his unique style of karaoke. Some human companions to these musical prodigies have developed a subtle group of hand signals so the Taurus dog will perform on cue.

You'll need patience and a loud, "No," to train your Taurus dog—but never angrily tell him to "shut up." He will never forgive you for using such boorish words. Calmly, yet sternly, let him know when he's wasting his water or barking at inappropriate times. A Taurus dog  appreciates discipline for two good reasons: He's eager to please you, and he enjoys any sort of attention focused on him.

Your Taurus would make a great nanny; he loves kids and is very protective. He safeguards family members without a moment's hesitation. He thinks and moves quickly, especially if children or grandparents are in danger. A Taurus dog's cosmic connection to your family tells him that certain family members need more sur-veillance than others. His show of concern may foreshadow a family member's ailment before there are any outward symptoms.

A Taurus dog is a real trooper. He's a dog to take fishing, camping, skiing, or on an all-day mountain trek. Have him help you select a Christmas tree, new rose bushes, or a Chia Pet. Take out some workout gear and let it sit in the room where he spends his days. He'll know you are at least planning some activity.

The Taurus dog has a phenomenal memory. His sharp ears pick up on tiny shifts in sounds. For example, your pup will point out that your heating or air-conditioning equipment is churning defectively. He will notice when you place your morning coffee cup down in a new way, or that you are upset when your favorite team loses a big game.

Symbol:
Bull, determined
and consistent

Taurus Pawcast

Ruling planet:
Venus, the planet of
beauty and pleasure

Key personality trait:

A Taurus dog possesses a hardy
disposition and stamina.

**Favorite
entertainment:**
listening to voices on
an answering machine
or a television

Dog idol:
Brahma bulldog,
firm and proud

Favorite activity with owner: singing

Favorite thing about owner: the way the house smells when you are baking or barbecuing, the mist that engulfs the bathroom after one of your long showers, and the way your houseplants create a natural environment

Pet peeves: throwing away his things and having to share

Dating style: Cautious. A Taurus dog generally makes friends after a watch-and-see period. He's loyal and typically sticks to one girl at a time, but he isn't opposed to playing the field every now and then. He's great with younger dog buddies.

Favorite sport:

fishing

Best feature:
patience

Worst feature:
digging in the garden

Dreams and fantasies: The Taurus dog dreams of living on a farm where he can herd cows or chickens or chase butterflies. You'll notice a Taurus dog because he will never hurt his animal playmates. He is able to hold things (birds and other small animals) without frightening or hurting them.

Would like more: Bird-watching. Get him something that restores his soul and reconnects him with nature such as a bird bath to attract birds to a window. The Taurus dog will spend many memorable, satisfying hours observing his feathery friends. Their singing pleases him, creating a little buzz in his throat, which may manifest as a hum. This is his sound of peaceful satisfaction.

Favorite food: chocolate

Mantra:

"I enjoy gracious living and enough food to make me fall asleep."

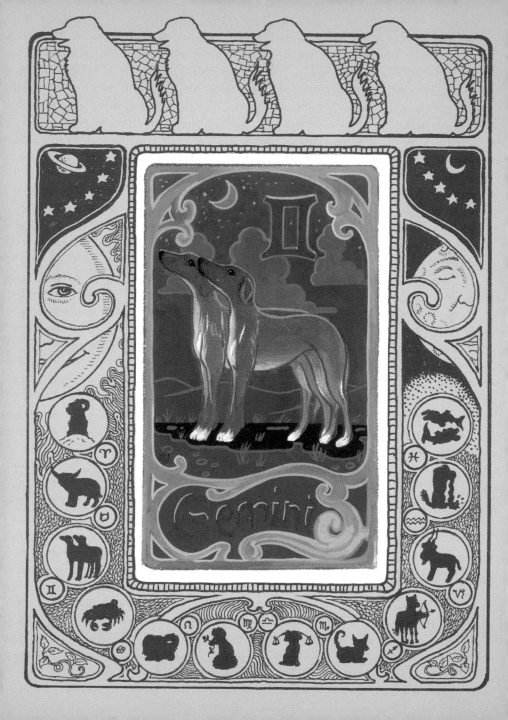

May 21—June 21

The
Gemini
Dog

G emini, the first air sign of the zodiac, has one of the fastest-thinking minds of canine partners. The Twins symbolize the Gemini sign and depict how versatile, multi-faceted, and complex she is. She is born able to read your mind and infer from your body language just what you are thinking. She often throws caution to the wind as she happily approaches new friends and neighbors or even tries to follow children to school. She is a great communicator and is naturally curious about her surroundings. You'll find it impossible to hide an impending trip from this curious pup by sneaking her travel crate out of your garage.

Secrets are an anathema to the nosey Gemini pooch. Her ideal job would be a gossip columnist or show business insider. Quite the fashionista, being trendy and up-to-date is more important to her than following in the classy footsteps of Audrey Hepburn. Your Gemini dog is always jumping, running, and getting water all over herself when she drinks from her bowl. Her good humor makes these antics cute and endearing, but if she saw others doing such things she'd run around the neighborhood tattling to her pals.

The crafty Gemini bonds with those who treat her well. She would handle a divorce in her family with the patience and understanding of a marriage counselor. Her divorcing human companions would no doubt fight for joint custody, but she'll be fine no matter which household she ends up in.

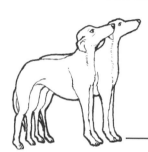 She'll miss the guardian she is not with, but she sees this as open season where the house rules can be changed permanently.

A Gemini dog is a master at playing one person against the other. One Gemini dog I knew conned three separate dinners from different family members each night, causing the mother to wonder why the pooch was gaining weight. This Gemini was caught open-mouthed on a nanny cam. Soon thereafter, she returned to her normal weight.

A Gemini is an opportunist. Leave the front gate open and this intellectually superior canine will turn adventurer. Make assumptions and she'll show you how wrong you are. Your Gemini dog is always up for some fun. Make her an integral part of your family's activities and take her with you whenever possible—she thrives on change and new people and places. Always let her have the last word. Whether with body language or a dramatic exit, the Gemini dog will feel that you respect her.

A Gemini never outgrows her puppylike attitude. When she gets older and you want to perk her up, simply talk about the good ol' days when she joined the family. She'll roll back time and, for a few minutes, feel young and frisky again.

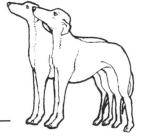

Gemini Pawcast

Symbol:
Twins, intelligent and versatile

Ruling planet:
Mercury, the planet of communication and day-to-day activities

Key personality trait:

A Gemini is always in the know, and you can expect she'll give her two cents on any topic.

Dog idol:
Lassie, tough and beautiful

Dreams and fantasies: A Gemini yearns to perform as she mingles with people and dog buddies. Her heaven would feature all sorts of warm, chopped beef with all the furniture she can chew.

Favorite activity with owner:

dancing to music or reading the latest fashion magazines

Favorite food:
warm, chopped beef

Best feature:
friendly

Worst feature:
tearing up
the lawn

Dating style:
Approachable. She's open to long, languid sniffs at home or in the park. She has a tendency to share her favors with many suitors; she makes a better friend than lover.

Pet peeves:
inactivity and repetition

Favorite sport: bounding over furniture and flying through the air, scurrying, flipping, and twisting

Favorite thing about owner: your friendliness and your insistence on taking her everywhere with you

---

Favorite entertainment:
sitting near the dinner table and watching television

Would like more:
Surprise. Boredom is the enemy! If you keep her guessing, she won't have time to be mischievous. She also likes it when you help her change her look. She likes trying out the newest doggy fashions, whether it's a scarf, collar, sweater or hat, she's not afraid to look silly. Above all, she just wants to have fun!

Mantra:

"You have only one mouth to fill. Go for anything not nailed down."

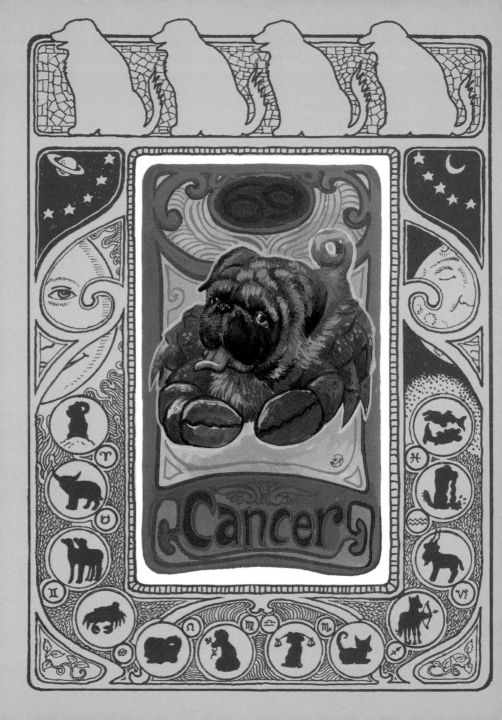

The Cancer Dog

A Cancer puppy is a domestic dream. Such a loving and cuddly creature, it's hard to imagine how your house could be a home without him curled up on the couch or stretched out by the fireplace. He completes a cozy picture —sometimes you'll swear he runs the place. He wakes everyone up on time, follows the gardener around, greets the mail carrier, and makes sure everyone is safe in their beds at night. If ever something seems a little off, he'll sound the alarm to make sure everyone checks out the potential infringement on his usually tranquil domicile.

He's often the first noticed when visitors come to your house, as he's very protective but not in an overt way. He likes to get close to newcomers and sense them out before he makes a sound. Intimidation is his specialty whether he's a toy poodle or a Great Dane. Sometimes he shows his love by bringing you creatures he's preyed upon outdoors, which could be upsetting for sensitive animal lovers. His gruesome gift is his way of telling you that he loves you so much that he'll share whatever he finds with you.

Your Cancer pup is ruled by the moon and is affected strongly by its daily changes. In a month's span he'll go from energetic to lethargic, happy to mopey, cranky to euphoric. He teaches us through his responsive temperament to be aware of atmospheric changes and to be pleased with what we can learn from each other. He's a constant reminder that all things are connected. Often he picks up on vibes in  the household. When people are having a good time, he adds to the fun. When they are upset, he'll be miserable too. It will amaze you that this pet is able to warn of things to come. He can predict earthquakes, floods, and hurricanes. He also senses subtle changes in your body chemistry, and lets you know he's worried, and this is an excellent time to see the doctor. This could be for happy occasions, too, such as a pregnancy!

A Cancer pooch wants you all to himself. He prefers that other pets give him his space. He's better with older animals of a different species than with young whipper-snappers who will tend to annoy him. Children aren't his favorite either. He can only put up with a little tugging and teasing and then will make it clear that the game is over. Perhaps it's best to keep the two separate. He loves music and wants you to turn the radio up while he lounges by the pool. Music and water together put him in a party mood—and he can howl at the moon like no other!

You and your Cancer canine have what can only be described as a parent-child bond. It is almost like you both are created with the same DNA code. So, of course, when you are distraught or feeling blue, the Cancer dog will pick up on this, and try his best to improve your situation.

Cancer Pawcast

Symbol:
Crab, a hard shell, but sensitive underside

Ruling planet:
moon, magnetically influential

Key personality trait:

Your Cancer dog is a moody pup, but you'll appreciate his sensitivity when you're not at your best either. Keeping a positive outlook will help keep this dog's demeanor pleasant.

Would like more:
time with you and the peaceful sound of running water

Dog idol:
dachshund, close to the ground and steady

Favorite activity with owner: receiving a scratch under the chin or on that spot behind the ear that's hard to reach

Favorite sport: water sports

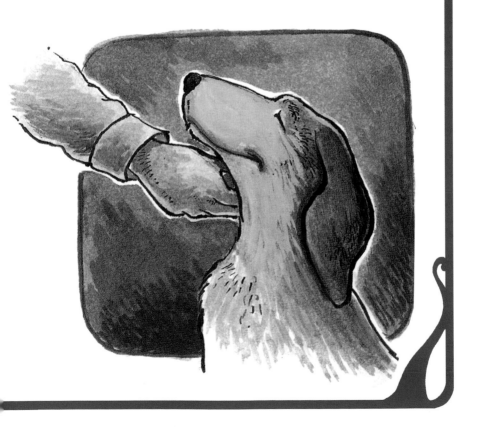

Dating style: Romantic. Your Cancer dog seeks a relationship with a top-of-the-line femme particularly interested in his company. No beating around the bush for this guy.

Best feature:
sweet heart
and integrity

Favorite thing about owner:

you're completely loveable, always happy, and always there for him

Worst feature:
killing
small animals

Favorite food:
deboned trout

Favorite entertainment:
live music

Pet peeves:
children's games

Dreams and fantasies: He dreams of running a big company. You would be amazed at this pup's mind for business. He has got a knack for supply and demand problems—he is very good at knowing what is needed and then providing it.

Mantra:
"Bring it on!"

July 23 — August 22

The Leo Dog

The Leo pup is a fire sign, ruled by the sun, with a roaring flame in her belly and a strong desire to please. Like her ruling planet, she quickly becomes the center of your universe and rewards you richly with unending affection when you orbit around her. Though the Leo loves to lazily bask in the sun, she's essentially a working dog. Give her a job, and she'll do it as long as she's sure you'll praise her when the job is done. She learns tricks quickly for the sheer enjoyment of being the center of attention, especially among your friends. She's less motivated by the treat you give her for rolling over than by the sound of applause from her fans.

Loyalty is one of the highest values held by your Leo. Even a Chihuahua puppy will be as fierce as a lion when it comes to protecting you. If you've got a larger breed Leo, take every precaution to make sure your canine bodyguard knows who's friend and who's foe. Make sure loved ones understand never to playfully roughhouse with you or they will likely meet with your pup's aggression.

Leos love dog competitions. Whether a purebred or a mixed breed, she behaves like royalty (as long as she thinks everyone is watching) when the pressure is on. She's no kiss-up, but she might give the judge a lick on the nose if she feels it's going to help her score. Her desire to win is strong! This pup is the alpha dog. If you have multiple pets, your Leo creature will fit right in with the rest, as long

as everyone respects her leadership. If not, it can get ugly. Leo is a bossy sign and any sass from other animals will incite her to

swipe, snarl, and nip her adversary into compliance. Of course, she prefers the company of dogs to cats, but you never have to worry about her being a danger to her feline friends.

She's terrific with kids as well, as Leo is the sign of children. For this reason, Leo dogs are very happy to be used for breeding purposes. Your Leo dog might tire you out with the endless amounts of energy, but this will be made bearable when she crashes out all night, not waking you up for a midnight snack or potty break. Of course she'd love to sleep in the bed with you—and you won't need an electric blanket with this hot-blooded pooch at the foot of your bed.

The Leo dog's profound sense of responsibility makes her want to protect you from harm. She'll anticipate the slightest deviation from your routine and immediately start pondering how she will be affected. After that self-preservation thought, she'll watch for a reason behind new behavior. A Leo has long psychic tentacles and, even when away from you, she will subconsciously reach out to warn you of any problems.

Leo
Pawcast

Symbol:
Lion, proud
and powerful

Ruling planet:
sun, the star we revolve around

Key personality trait:

A Leo loves to perform. Reward her
with praise and she'll be the star of
the show at any get-togethers at
your home.

**Favorite
entertainment:**
chasing and playing
with tiny animals
or toys

Dog idol:
mastiff,
lordly and
brave

Dreams and fantasies: You might be surprised to know that your Leo dog has dreams of show biz. She loves the camera, but mostly comes to life in front of an audience— the bigger the better. If ever there is an opportunity to get her mug on film, whether it be the a home movie of a birthday party or a commercial for your neighborhood car dealership, she'll be a stunner at the audition.

Dating style: Family-focused. She prefers to think past friendly formalities and get on with having a litter.

Best feature:
loyalty and generosity

Favorite thing about owner:

your sweet aroma after a shower

Favorite activity with owner:

camping

Worst feature:
devilish in testing your good sense of humor

Would like more:

Choices. A Leo loves the constant activity of everyone going this way and that. This gives her more choices—do I stay home or go to the store with my friend? Do I follow Junior to school or watch soap operas with Grandma? Even if she's not invited to join these activities, she thinks she is. She loves watching and partaking in the daily endless decision making.

Favorite food:
home-cooked dinners

Pet peeves:

laziness and routine

Favorite sport:
admiring herself

Mantra:

"If it's not the best, it's not for me."

VIRGO

The Virgo Dog

Never was there a dog more suited to live with humans than a Virgo—he might even be cleaner, more orderly, and more domesticated than the humans he shares a home with! With all life's hustle and bustle, we can learn from the way he creates order in his world. What's most important to the Virgo pup is pleasing his master. He strives to be perfect in your eyes and quickly ascertains your expectations so that he can fulfill them. If this pup is a little high-strung it's only because he's trying so hard to please you. Ruled by Mercury, (the planet named for the ancient god of communication) you'll swear he understands every word you say. The frustrating part for him is that you don't understand his language. The Virgo dog needs to know you are trying to "get" him; he will communicate with you more clearly if he feels you are receptive.

This is the tidiest dog you've ever seen. Notice how he puts his toys in the same spot every time. He's got a system and he sticks to it. He is concerned about personal hygiene and he's constantly preening himself—but don't let that dissuade you from taking him to a professional groomer; it's the highlight of his month! He adores being fluffed and freshened and even likes getting his teeth cleaned.

Young or old, this is one dog who is always up for learning a new trick. He picks things up quickly as long as

your instructions are consistent. If not, he could get cranky and irritated by your confusing commands. He really hates when misunderstandings keep him from performing at the top of his game. The Virgo dog feels best with a firm routine. He's not a spontaneous creature. Leaving this dog at home when you travel can disrupt his psyche. Try leaving him with the same dog-sitting service each time so he won't be as flustered.

Virgo dogs are usually very healthy. They often survive beyond their typical life expectancy. If you have a choice in medical treatments, they prefer holistic remedies. Virgos love to flaunt their youthful glow. If an elderly Virgo dog lives with a younger pup, the older dog will be too competitive to not participate in activities with the same enthusiasm as his young counterpart. It's one way to keep your Virgo dog happy in his senior years.

The Virgo dog appears to be a know-it-all. You can almost sense he's trying to play with your mind as he seems to understand what you want him to do. A Virgo can often put two and two together faster than you can. He sees in his mind's eye what the outcome of a situation will be. The way he greets you at the end of the day speaks volumes—his thoughts often mirror the deep secrets you carry.

Virgo Pawcast

Symbol:
The Virgin, pure and modest

Ruling planet:
Mercury, the planet of communication and day-to-day events

Key personality trait:

A Virgo pup thrives when you respect his need for consistency and routine. He's a quick learner and daily practice allows him to master any trick. Be understanding that he needs clear instruction.

Dog idol:
coyote, an adaptable survivor

Favorite thing about owner:

your kind attention,
patience, and laziness

Favorite food:
lamb

Favorite activity with owner:
grooming

Dating style:

Low-key. Your Virgo prefers a quiet night at home rather than a noisy park with lots of loose pooches invading his space. He enjoys the loyalty of one to the admiration of the pack.

Best feature:
tidiness

Worst feature:
high maintenance

Pet peeves:

when you haven't cleaned up the house, fleas, and when his toys are out of order

Favorite sport:
being brushed

Would like more:
long walks, smart-looking bandanas, and trips to the vet for a checkup

Favorite entertainment:
watching clumsy, silly humans

Dreams and fantasies:
The Virgo mentally escapes to a day spa where he enjoys a manicure and a canine massage.

Mantra:
"Where there is chaos, I bring calm."

September 23—October 23

The Libra Dog

T he fall equinox signals the start of the Libra sign, the time when the crops have been harvested but there are still some vestiges of the summer's warmth. This seventh sign of the zodiac begins the six-month cycle of the year when cooperation with others is essential for survival. Libras need to be around people and other living creatures to be happy. Your Libra dog is a team player. She craves appreciation and will perform Herculean feats just to gain a pat on the head. But she is not a passive partner; she's a genius at forming coalitions. A Libra is a natural political player and is the perfect dog to bring to the office. She will help you gain the favor of the higher-ups and key clients, helping you save face and gain respect.

Libra is sometimes called the marriage sign because bonds—whether romantic, platonic, or familial—are what make those of this sign tick. Just as a wife can aid a husband's career and lifestyle, or a supportive husband can bolster a wife's ambitions, the Libra dog does the same for her beloved human companion. Your pup wants to brag about her affiliation with you and your family. Expect her excitement when referred to as the Jones' dog. Don't think she doesn't know your names. When Mom calls out for Joanne, the Libra dog will immediately look at Joanne. Should Mom be angry with Dad, your Libra will warn him of trouble brewing in the kitchen. However, should she get herself in a little hot water, she will run under the bed to

hide—Libras really hate to be yelled at. Threats of punishment fall on deaf ears. To get through to a Libra dog, the only method that works is presenting a logical argument while stroking her head. Libra is the sign of balance, symbolized by the Scales of Justice. She will only decide what to do when presented with the options, and she must get a sense that you are open to negotiation. Unfortunately, Libras are not fast decision makers. Multiple choices only confuse her, so offer her only two options.

A Libra enjoys the niceties of life: a warm blanket, preferably cashmere; a gourmet dog treat; and elegant beauty parlors. She would never embarrass you with offensive behavior, except when she overhears your bedroom romps. She'll barge right in—hopefully your bed partner is a pet lover, or you'll end up telling yourself that you care more about your pooch than a lover anyway. Your Libra pet companion will score another triumph. As you hug her, neither of you hears the slamming of the front door.

The Libra dog was born to be an active part of your home. She instinctively senses your mood and responds accordingly. She understands when changes in the home disrupt the peace. She can smell fear or trauma and knows when to approach you.

Libra Pawcast

Symbol:
Scales, for balance and justice

Ruling planet:
Venus, the planet of pleasure and beauty

Key personality trait:

A Libra pup will stick by her owner's side through the ups and downs of life.

Dog idol:
bloodhound, for compassion and justice

Dreams and fantasies: Your Libra whimpers as she dreams of food dishes overflowing with hamburger and dog cookies on a couch with her owner.

Favorite thing about owner:

your constant chatter;
and your hugs, tail
tugs, and when you
pick her up

Favorite food:
hamburger

Favorite activity with owner:

tumbling through the sections of Sunday's newspaper as you try to read

Best feature:
wet nose

Pet peeves:
yelling and disruption of balance within the home and people who are sneaky and unfair

Worst feature:
hates to do tricks and work

Favorite entertainment: being petted by several folks at one time

Would like more: long walks and socializing time in dog parks

Dating style: Social. She longs to be desired by an attractive Gemini pooch. A Libra is easy-going and loves the search for a perfect mate, though she's more interested in just plain being part of a couple.

Mantra:

"I can handle my life and yours."

SCORPIO

October 23—November 21

The Scorpio Dog

This pup is a lover, not a fighter—unless someone is threatening you. Passionate and jealous, your Scorpio dog wants your attention and will richly reward you for giving it. His chief offering is to be a constant, loyal, protective, and affectionate fixture in your life. Scorpios make excellent breeders, as Scorpio is the sign of inheritance and character. Your Scorpio will hand down his best qualities and if he is a purebred; the litter that comes from his genes will be especially impressive and surpass the standards of his pedigree. If you do not intend your Scorpio dog to breed, then it's best not to take any chances in this department. A Scorpio in heat is quite resourceful when it comes to breaking out and finding a mate.

This puppy has a sneaky side, which is part of his charm. When you think you can predict his behavior, he'll surprise you, reminding you that you're not the only smart one around. There are bones hidden in your yard, toys hidden in your closet, and that pair of shoes you thought you'd lost is probably chewed up and buried under the house. None of these actions was intended to upset you; his creative nature drives these projects and this may never make sense to human beings.

Make sure your pup always has clean water because a Scorpio dog has a sensitive urinary tract. Make sure he can always go out when he needs to, which is often. He's a candidate for the doggy door, and having one could add years to his life.

Scorpios make excellent police dogs. They outclass others in sniffing out narcotics and finding a missing person. Their favorite job is digging, but humans seldom have a need for that one. In fact, if there's a sprinkler to be dug up, watch out. If your leave your Scorpio dog home alone, you may have extra yard work to do later. He is obsessed with unearthing things. To prevent this kind of trouble, try adding another dog to your family. The more there is to do and think about, the less trouble your Scorpio will get into.

The best treat for a Scorpio is a trip to the beach. Playing along the shore is his idea of heaven. He's a good swimmer and feels invigorated by the challenge of being in the water. He also loves to play with you, but not only ordinary games like catch and tug-of-war; he likes a good puzzle, too. Hide a bone in the house and see how long it takes him to find it. He'll soon have you convinced that he's psychic!

The Scorpio dog envisions what is going on and upcoming in his beloved human companion's life. Do you ever wonder what your Scorpio is daydreaming about? You. He sees you living a glorious life and pictures himself enjoying it with you. When trouble is near, the Scorpio has the psychic savvy to help you circumvent disaster.

Scorpio Pawcast

Symbol:
Scorpion, mysterious and intense

Ruling planet:
Pluto, planet of regeneration and secrets

Key personality trait:

The Scorpio dog always has his owner on his mind.

Dreams and fantasies:
He dreams of being pursued on a beach or park by a pack of smitten canines. He also dreams of a wild birthday party with twenty of his closest pals in attendance.

Dog idol:
fox, for its Machiavellian nature

Favorite activity with owner:
hide and seek

Dating style: Adventurous. He seeks aggressive, romantic dogs in the neighborhood.

Best feature: sexy crawl

Favorite thing about owner:

your willingness to take him along

Worst feature: waking in the wee morning hours

Pet peeves: being restrained on a leash and having his name called constantly

Favorite entertainment: soft music with the smell of incense in the background

| **Favorite food:** |
| steak |

Would like more:

Humor. Your companion has a wicked sense of humor. Catching you unaware with a zinger of visual jokes is a favorite thing for your Scorpio to do, and he rests easier knowing he has made you laugh. Next to tickling your funny bone, this furry friend enjoys warming your heart with a good dose of poignancy. Like the Scorpion's sting, your friend can stun you by touching you just where you're most vulnerable— your emotions.

| **Favorite sport:** |
| beach volleyball |

Mantra:

"Don't be bashful."

The Sagittarius Dog

Your Sagittarian pooch may have been a stray dog who found you, as many of this sign are restless as youngsters who break free to see the world. Even if you purchased your pup at a pet store, you can be certain it was not you who chose her, but the opposite. She's the best friend you'll ever have, and you will take her everywhere with you. She loves nothing more than to travel in the car, by boat, or by plane. She's got a winning personality, and she makes friends wherever she goes. In fact, she's introduced you to a few fresh faces—some furry, some human. When it's time to venture out, she's absolutely fearless.

A Sagittarian prefers the great outdoors whenever possible and being let off the leash is the highlight of her day. She needs to be walked twice as much as other dogs; making sure she stays active will give her a longer life. It seems she always wants to go out, even when you don't! You'll have to keep a really sturdy fence around her in order to keep her safe. This is one dog who needs to have her tags on her at all times!

Even if your dog is not bred to be a bird dog or pointer, she is adept at making you notice things. She is drawn to anything unusual and unique and is always quick to bring to your attention strange things around you. You'll have to keep her from eating the random flora and fauna she feels

compelled to sample—she's not the best at staying away from things that are bad for her; at least she's not afraid to try something new. Have you ever seen a pack of dogs tearing down the street together, investigating the world at warp speed? Sagittarius leads the pack. She loves an expedition and tells other dogs where they need to go. Your Sagittarius dog doesn't like to be confronted and she'll growl ferociously toward those who question her authority.

She doesn't like being groomed, but she'll tolerate it, especially if you go to a different groomer every once in a while. She'll be on her best behavior when she's around new people. She prefers a short, no-nonsense cut because of her active lifestyle. Her favorite people are children, or people who aren't afraid to act like children. She's imaginative and playful; she enjoys the fact that kids are always changing and growing. Since she gets bored easily, she responds well to challenges. She's extremely trainable, loves to learn, and remembers what she's taught.

The Sagittarian dog is the great truth-teller and truth-seeker. She will be your psychic guide and moral compass. A Sagittarius knows what is right and will pierce the defenses of anyone who challenges her beloved human companion.

Sagittarius Pawcast

Symbol:
Archer, directed with high aims

Ruling planet:
Jupiter, planet of luck and abundance

Key personality trait:

This playful pup can be quite bossy, but know it's mostly due to her protective nature.

Dog idol:
Rin Tin Tin, always there for you

Dreams and fantasies: A Sagittarius dog dreams of journeying to the moon. She is intrigued by space travel and is courageous enough to go anywhere.

Best feature: She's a lucky charm. Born under the sign of luck and abundance, all you have to do is pat her head or rub her belly and you get an extra charge of good fortune. Bring your pup to a poker game or sneak her in your purse when you're going to an important meeting.

Dating style: Explores greener pastures. She'll go over the fence to run with different breeds. She involves herself with other pooches' love interests while ignoring her own significant other.

Favorite sport:

staying three steps ahead of you

Worst feature: jumping on humans

Favorite food: top-of-the-line canned meat

Favorite activity with owner: embarking on a trip to a new dog park

Favorite thing about owner: When you switch up her doggy shampoo, you surprise her with a new collar.

Would like more: Variety. A Sagittarius feels that one way to show affection is to keep the relationship lively and unpredictable. If playing catch was the big game last month, your pup will show an interest in chasing frogs this month. Next month's hobby might be jogging. This is one puppy who never wants you to get bored of the companionship you share.

Favorite entertainment:
chasing cars

Pet peeves:
not enough sitting space in front of windows and too much brushing

Mantra:

"My master's best friend on land, sea, or air."

CAPRICORN

The Capricorn Dog

The Capricorn sign begins on the first day of the winter solstice, a magical window that provides dogs with physical and mental stamina and fortitude. With long nights and short days, your Capricorn instinctively learns about time—how to sense it, use it, and flow with events. He is an old soul with wisdom far beyond his years. His mind is so powerful that other animals with seniority obey his demands. The Capricorn can be very easygoing on petty things, but should his food or water be threatened, this sign will stand his ground regardless of pleas. Tell the Capricorn that a couch or a room is off-limits and when you're least expecting it, he will sleep on your satin cushions. Company coming? The Capricorn will sense an important guest and will decide that this is the occasion to be the household spokesman. At the appropriate moment, this dog will demonstrate how his owner feels about the visitor.

Capricorn dogs like to work. Sure, you can fetch the paper yourself, but this pooch thrives on any routine that brings you two into daily contact. Remember he is time sensitive. He'll wake up from a nap just before the kids come home from school or start demanding attention when you are least able to give it.

Capricorn dogs have a special relationship with the phone. When it rings they'll suddenly need to be let out. Or

if they're outside they may decide to start unearthing and relocating your plants to show you that they know you're unable to get out there. Senior family members are especially important to the Capricorn dog.

You'll think your dog has eyes in the back of his head as he suddenly races to the side of a sick family member.

Out of all the signs, the Capricorn hates to visit the vet the most. He'll howl, scream, and carry on with an Academy Award–winning performance. He'll calm down—unless he has to wait. Waiting brings out the beast in your pup. Therefore, an early morning appointment is best.

The Capricorn has a long life thanks to his hearty constitution. He is a mentor to young pups, teaching them all he knows—both good and bad. Whether young or old, a Capricorn dog has a wild libido. "The more the merrier," the Capricorn says; maybe that's the secret to his longevity.

The Capricorn dog's psychic nature leaves him more attuned to your mental commands than your vocal ones. If you tell him to stop behaving badly, he won't if he senses that a part of you is secretly laughing at his silliness. His strong feelings regarding territory and family are commanding and his sense of direction is superb. He can help you find your way when you feel you are lost.

Capricorn Pawcast

Symbol:
Goat, leaping past obstacles to the top

Ruling planet:
Saturn, the planet of life lessons and discipline

Key personality trait:

A Capricorn pup wants to be useful. He enjoys helping out around the house with activities such as waking up the children.

Dog idol:
hyena, for determination and loyalty

Favorite thing about owner:
your appreciation of his need for individual attention

Would like more: Style. Capricorns care about status. Their accessories don't have to be lavish, but they must be classy and refined. Forget the glitter and get out your Capricorn gold. His pet identification tag must be unobtrusive and practical. His bowl doesn't have to be overly pretty, just really clean.

Dating style: Selective. He searches for a loyal mate who has similar traits and discipline, and who enjoys quality food.

Best feature:
Long-term thinker. He will protect you from unworthy suitors, ensuring that you make the correct choice.

Favorite sport: retrieving the newspaper

Worst feature: sometimes a bit melodramatic

Pet peeves: waiting, clutter, ridicule, and too much sun

Dreams and fantasies:
Staying in good shape despite how much food is heaped on his plate is a dream for this pup.

Favorite activity with owner:
grooming, bathing, and similar routine tasks

Favorite food:
meaty bones

Favorite entertainment:
bringing you the leash for his morning walk

Mantra:
"Work makes you happy."

January 20—February 18

The Aquarius Dog

You've seen plenty of Aquarius dogs on television who like to show off their strange and wonderful tricks, many of them self-taught. They like to think up their own tricks and then teach you (and you are merely the assistant). Aquarius dogs are inventors, always creating ways to amuse themselves and others. Your Aquarius is one quick puppy. She zooms around from room to room, over hills and mountains, always happiest when out of breath.

Sometimes she darts underfoot, which is dangerous for both of you. You'll have to watch out for her because she's not watching out for you. She's too focused on the butterfly or ball she's chasing. Running after cars is one of her guilty pleasures, so always keep her leashed near streets. A social creature, she enjoys having people around. Invite her to your parties and she'll make the rounds, kissing babies like a politician and letting people pet her. If you really want to give her a present, throw a party in her honor! Invite people, dogs, and even cats—she's very open-minded when it comes to choosing friends. She's even been known to socialize with the likes of possums and skunks.

Somewhat of a canine philanthropist, she's suited to working alongside humans, especially if they are in need of rescue. She's not as afraid of fire, smoke, water, or snow as other creatures are and will have amazing stamina in adverse conditions (as long as she's got enough water to drink). She was born under the sign of the Water Bearer, who gives the gift of life.

Her fast metabolism makes her very hungry, and she might even have a begging problem. She can't stand when everyone is eating except her and she'll vocalize this. To fix the issue, feed her at the same time that you eat and in the same room, too. She's got a hearty appetite and will eat the strangest table scraps. Since she's not picky, it's up to you to make sure nobody gives her anything she shouldn't have, especially anything with sugar in it. She's easygoing in a multi-pet household. Since she feels she's got nothing to prove, the usual territorial issues don't apply, but she does want to be treated as an equal who shares your home. If she's not allowed on the couch or bed, make sure she's got her own cushion or blanket to compensate. As long as she knows you appreciate her, she won't complain or behave badly. She loves to bark and will go on for hours if nobody is home. For this reason it is best if she's not an only dog. The more pet friends she has, the easier it will be on the neighbors!

The Aquarian dog is a futurist. She knows the environment you are living in and is quite practical in her needs, wants, and communications. She can project her thoughts (actually she uses picture images) on to you as well as others. Foes turn into allies when this friendly Aquarius is around.

Aquarius Pawcast

Symbol:
Water Bearer, a giver of life

Ruling planet:
Uranus, the planet of surprises and of the unpredictable

Key personality trait:

There's no sitting still for an Aquarius pup. She'll love to tag along with you on all your errands and still have energy for a game of fetch.

Dog idol:
whippet, for speed and endurance

Dreams and fantasies: She dreams of being a lifeguard for her owner, being sure only good things happen within the household.

Favorite activity with owner: a motorcycle ride and listening to you practice your favorite musical instrument

Best feature:
friendliness

Dating style:
Casual. She prefers a knockabout relationship with another vigorous canine—not necessarily of the same size or breed.

Favorite thing about owner:

that you allow her to socialize with visitors

Pet peeves:
a house that's too quiet

Worst feature:
Nonstop barking, especially if she is an only pup. She loves to sing, but others don't appreciate it. Your Aquarius also likes to make dog friends who you may not approve of just to push your buttons.

Favorite sport:

roughing it up with
the nearest pet or person

**Favorite
entertainment:**
barking, running, and
chasing moving objects

Would like more:
Color. An Aquarius dog
is into dog fashion
trends. She loves
color—even though it is
believed that dogs are
colorblind. Beware:
hard-wired in her genes
is a fear of uniforms—
and the people who
wear them.

Favorite food:
lean beef

Mantra:

"Mischief and speed belong together."

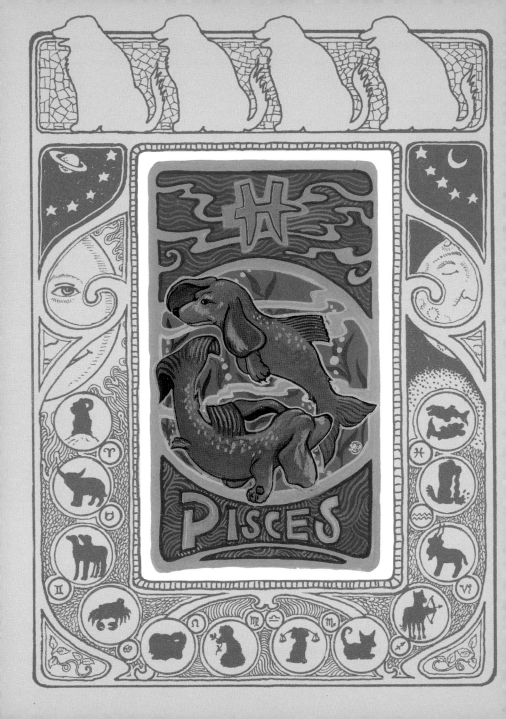

PISCES

February 19—March 20

The Pisces Dog

Y ou've thought he was an angel sent from heaven in canine form, and you could be right. He seems to connect with you on many levels. Though you are of different species, the two of you have many common interests and shared pursuits that help make you both better creatures in the world. This pup is a wise soul. You'll feel you are learning from him and wonder whether you are taking care of him, or if he is taking care of you.

Born under the sign of the Fish, the Pisces dog is very sensitive. He's aware of even subtle changes in the environment, especially humidity and weather; the elements affect him more than most dogs. If your dog is a Pisces, it's likely that he has weird allergies. You may have to change his food often until you figure out what best fits his delicate digestive system to protect his sensitive tummy.

The upside of his sensitive nature is that the Pisces dog is always in tune with your moods. It makes him happy to nuzzle up to you when you're feeling cuddly, or yip and bounce when you need to be more energetic. If ever you're sad or sick, he's a healer and a helper. His wet nose and beautiful eyes are always a comfort.

His strange habits and idiosyncrasies add to his character. Though they don't make sense to people, these are behavioral patterns that serve a definite purpose in his  world. Try and see things from his point of view to figure out why he behaves the way he does. You might find it difficult to believe, but your Pisces puppy often dreams of seeing the world from your point of view. He finds your behaviors curious and fascinating.

A Pisces pup is the ideal mate for seniors. His mellow, intuitive nature makes him easy to care for, and his funny quirks make him a delight to have around. There will always be a funny story to share about his latest antics.

He prefers to sleep at the foot of your bed, but don't worry—he won't get up several times a night or fidget and fuss until he wakes you up. Dreamland is one of his favorite stomping grounds, so once his head hits the pillow he's out like a light!

The Pisces dog has the special ability to tap into the universal unconscious (think Carl Jung) and discover secrets that have been hidden for years. Need help finding a lost object? The Pisces is your dog detective. He has unbounded creativity and he can help you bring out your creativity. A day at the beach or lounging near a lake will turn your Pisces pal into the muse you've always sought.

Pisces Pawcast

Symbol:
Fish, riding
the currents

Ruling planet:
Neptune, the planet of
dreams and illusions

Key personality trait:

His sensitive
nature makes this
dog attuned to
his owner's
emotional needs.

Dog idol:
Pluto, for
being gentle
and kind

Favorite activity with owner:
sharing plenty of off-leash chases

Worst feature: He is picky about being trained and will resist doing a trick until he decides the time is right. He loudly drinks from the water bowl at all times of the day and night. A Pisces dog also has a special affinity with mud. He loves to trek through it and often comes into the house after a rainstorm covered in brown dirt. However, he does not like grease or being messy; it is just that he feels a special connection with the earth and water.

Dating style: Fussy. He demands a mate with similar finicky characteristics. He's a follower with a young body; an older, more organized mind would do.

Favorite food:
ground beef
in gravy

Pet peeves:

a noisy room
and the roar
of a passing
motorcycle

Favorite thing about owner:

your laughter

Best feature:
accepting
your offbeat
habits

Would like more: regularity in feeding and play time

Dreams and fantasies: Your Pisces pup dreams of living on a lake or, better yet, at the marina on a boat. He is not a hardworking dog; he appreciates a life of contemplation and observation and he expects luxury items.

Favorite sport: running along the beach

Favorite entertainment:

trekking through mud

Mantra:

"I think, therefore I am."

YOUR DOG'S

IDEAL
PET OWNER

Conclusion

I t's only fitting that you pamper your dog as you would yourself by capitalizing on her Petrological sun sign. You can ease your dog's life and improve her personality by working through her sign's basic characteristics. You'll further appreciate your pet's virtual psychic ability—such as her knack of responding to your sadness, anger, or loneliness. She can sense earthquakes and extreme weather changes.

Aries. An Aries dog appreciates a proud owner who can wrestle and respond when she's in the mood to play. The energetic Aries needs an owner who doesn't mind repeating training requirements, accepts strong territorial instincts, and her desire to be the center of attention.

Taurus. The Taurus dog loves a homebody guardian, and children who smother him with affection. It's helpful if this dog owner allows crawling on furniture and doesn't mind occasional accidents during long separations. Thoughtful between-meal snacks will definitely build a bond between owner and pooch.

Gemini. A friendly, petting-conscious, active guardian will put this pup on cloud nine. Car rides are also appreciated. An owner who can put up with her tendency to wander and finicky appetite makes this dog's life complete.

Cancer. The cancer dog is attracted to an owner—preferably female—who believes she can communicate nonverbally with her pet. He appreciates a very clean and quiet home life as top dog, warmed by lots of human attention.

Leo. A Leo is a good watchdog for a loving household. She constantly tests her owner with noisy actions, desiring playful interaction. Leo dogs make excellent "substitute" children.

Virgo. Virgo dogs are great buddies for independent, unstructured owners. They enjoy being home with their owners—as long they each have their own spaces. Owners who enjoy cool weather with access to other small animals ring the bells of Virgo pups.

Libra. The Libra pooch feels most comfortable in the company of a patient owner couple. She may even need the presence of another pet. She lives for human touching, grooming, and leaning against you. She loves an owner who'll share the bed.

Scorpio. This dog responds well to a dominant owner with an appreciation of ESP. The guardian of this hound must value a loyal and very possessive significant furry friend who senses his owner's every move. An ideal owner will have a yard and children.

Sagittarius. A Sag dog dwells well with an owner who doesn't mind a curious, nosey pooch—in and outside your home. She plays better with adults than children. The best Sagittarius owner will be a careful driver around this dog.

Capricorn. The Capricorn canine is a wonderful watchdog for a single owner who may be absent a great deal as long as there's easy access to a yard. This finicky dog has a recurring interest in climbing his patient owner's low fence.

Aquarius. The Aquarius pooch is a wonderful addition to a big family. Children and teens are the answer to this dog's play dreams. Owners who teach tricks will mix well with an Aquarius, as do owners with other pets.

Pisces. Guardians who appreciate clean and fastidious dogs will love the Pisces. A regular feeding schedule is necessary for Pisces pups. An owner must make sure his Pisces pet doesn't overheat and is always cuddled.

Lunar cycles promote new relationships, especially with animals. When you decide to introduce a new dog in your home, you may wish to do so during a new moon, the first quarter of the lunar month. Most newspapers and almanacs list this information for your convenience.

By becoming your dog's ideal pet owner, you will be able to communicate better with your pup and create a healthier living environment for the entire family. Be sure to incorporate your pooch into your daily activities to make her feel like a true family member. You can do this by signing your dog's name—or her paw print—on birthday cards, by getting "from our dog to your dog" holiday cards, or by including your dog when asked the number of family members in your household. These small, considerate actions will make you an ideal pet owner.

Understanding your dog's astrology is the first step toward a better life with her. So learn how to keep the stars in mind for a better future with your dog.